Inexhaustible Offering
Lincoln Park Mornings

Inexhaustible Offering

LINCOLN PARK MORNINGS

Poems by
CAROLYN KELLEY WILLIAMS

Paintings by
LILY GAINES

Copyright © 2020 by Carolyn Kelley Williams
Paintings © 2020 Lily Gaines

Cover and interior design by Masha Shubin | Inkwater.com

All rights reserved. No part of this book may be reproduced or transmitted in any form or by any means whatsoever, including photocopying, recording or by any information storage and retrieval system, without written permission from the publisher and/or author.

Paperback ISBN 978-1-7352115-0-3
eBook   ISBN 978-1-7352115-1-0

3 5 7 9 10 8 6 4

For Fred

Contents

WINTER INTO SPRING

Lake Michigan 3
Joy 4
From Diversey Harbor 5
Crow, Spring 6
Do Not Bring Sorrow Here 7
How Transformation Comes 8
Equinox Approaches 9
I Wake to Rain 10

SPRING INTO SUMMER

Morning Lesson 15
Music 16
Waiting for God to Appear 17
Riding Forth 18
The Trees 19
Dialogue 20

SUMMER INTO AUTUMN

City and Lake 25
August Again 26
After Two Weeks with Mary Oliver 27
Storm 28
Concerning the Kingdom of God 30
Belmont Harbor 31
At Water's Edge 32
End of Summer 33
Autumn Haze 34

AUTUMN INTO WINTER

Painterly 39
Basics 40
Melancholy 41
Chill. 42
Essentials 43
Offering 44
Illumination 45

About the Artists 47
Acknowledgements 49

Inexhaustible Offering
Lincoln Park Mornings

WINTER INTO SPRING

Lake Michigan

Morning after morning
I make my pilgrimage to the lake.

Never mind that instead of reflected temples
streaks of condominium undulate among the blues.

Never mind that this is an inland waterway,
glacier-formed and, relatively speaking, young.

The vast waters disappearing beyond the horizon
cannot be adequately spoken of.

The sun glinting off the surface
cannot be looked at directly.

In matters of spirit we must be cautious
of the particular:
Call this boundless abundance
endlessly changing,
ever the same,
Source.

Joy

I go out looking for my life.

I see at once
everywhere in the gardens
winter grasses, parched,
broken.

I think of Ecclesiastes,
how my life
is like those grasses.

Then bounding across the lawn
comes a dog,
caring nothing for Ecclesiastes,
clearly willing to be happy forever.

Now some ducks in the lagoon
trail their seven half-grown children,
instructing them on miracles
under the surface.

Even the gulls, rather monkish at the shore,
suddenly fling themselves into the wind
with what surely is a hallelujah.

Do you think joy
is a choice we make
day after day
to be like the ducks, the gulls,
the dog, barking wildly now,
retrieving a tossed ball
again and again and again
from the waves?

From Diversey Harbor

Across the water,
the fabled city: El Dorado.

I sit on the rocks.
A dinghy swings around.
Gulls utter rusty cries.

My spirit raises its sails
and pushes off,
Magellan, Columbus,
toward new worlds,
whatever imagination
sees as possible
on the far shore.

Crow, Spring

The person standing on the shore notices
that the crow, huge, harsh-voiced,
argumentative as a whiskeyed matron,
is too heavy for the sapling,
bends the branch almost to breaking
before lurching off
and thumping up into the mist.

Looking closely, the person sees
that the branch is, in fact, not skeletal,
is laden with nubs like little furry antlers
or fists full of dollar bills
aching to be spent.

The person, walking now along the water's edge,
is aching to be spent, too. But this early in the season,
possibilities are wadded and tight, like buds,
and most of the action is within; and everything—
two fishermen casting lines from shore,
quiescent lake, becoming mist, rising,
fish, like hope, breaking the surface,
sharp green knives of jonquils slicing
through the crust of earth—
everything seems imminent.

But the cardinals, whistling,
announce: *We have blossomed.*
We are already everything we need to be.

Do Not Bring Sorrow Here

Lake, a milky arc,
darkens, stipples.

Tan sand recalls:
Rain hit hard.
Walkers were here.

Grasses lay shadows
away from the sun,
which lifts itself slowly.

Behind the shore,
chiming in the woods—
thrushes, finches, cardinals.

Sit near the dune.
Become a stone smoothed
by time, by water moving.
Become a shell, driftwood,
fragment of bone.

How Transformation Comes

And so I go out into another morning,
head full of questions.

A perfect day.
The grass, which yesterday seemed
dead and unpromising, is strewn with birds
discovering something wondrous.

On the shore,
pigeons and gulls by the hundreds,
sorted according to white or gray,
all facing the same way
until two lanky dogs gallop into their midst,
stirring a flurry of wings.

Look! Sun on water:
Sequins on teal crepe,
foil, shaken;
diamonds, certainly,
and quicksilver,
starfire.

Is this how transformation comes?
Not by reason or argument.

Maybe if you allow yourself
to be dazzled, questions
simply fall away.

Equinox Approaches

Cosmic upheaval, unfathomable, vast,
as our already mighty star,
intensified, flares out,
strikes satellites dumb.

Winter's end.
Upheavals of our own;
yearnings, passions, bursting of constraints.
Night, for an instant, equals day.

Ah! Spring pours forth.
Waxing of luscious light.
Rain-caresses. Sumptuous odors.
Gardens lavish with greens.

Fishes, awakening in murky depths,
swim free. Water sparkles.
Worms press upward;
chicks burst shells.

The Sun God, ardent, stretches out his hand.
Dark Maiden from the Realm of Shadows, Kore,
ripe with desire, steps into the light. They dance.
Their footprints flower.

I Wake to Rain

All night, rain has streamed across windows,
even into the house, streaking walls,
dripping off shutters,
brazenly dropping onto the bed.

Loving this wildness
I hurry out to the lake, eager
for thunder more felt than heard,
wands of fire thrusting.

Even at a distance
I see waves exploding,
shore-trees shaken,
birds swept this way and that.

In time, the storm
sweeps everything away—
sky, shore, waves, lake, birds, trees,
towering city. Vanished.

Sated and drenched, I head home
through streets awhirl with water.
How good to pour such intensity
into the ordinary.

SPRING INTO SUMMER

Morning Lesson

I want to love the morning,
love this animal body. But my dreams
must have had some sorrow in them.
Even the sky, usually so optimistic,
seems a bit morose.

Making my way around the lagoon
I arrive at my usual bench. I sit.

Where is the lesson?

Nothing much happens until ducks,
some thirty of them, head over from the island
and, directly in front of me, offer this:
Slip easily into your life.
Let it carry you.

From several dogs at water's edge:
Plunge into your life.
Drink of it heartily.
Shake it off with musical sounds,
glitters of light.

Music

Last night, storm:
Kettle drums, snare drums,
cymbals crashing together—
all the percussions. More to come,
from the freighted look
of the gray, now tacit, sky.

In the trees, piccolos, flutes.
Clarinets across the lagoon.
Off to the left, saxophone,
jazz trumpet through a mute:
A wailing dog's complaint.

I think about losing my hearing,
how I love the voice
of every instrument,
the music of all these voices.

I listen as though my life
depended upon it.
I imagine it does.

Waiting for God to Appear

Eighteenth century Sweden.
Someone goes into a church and says,
I will wait here until God appears to me.

This morning I sit by the lagoon,
thinking much the same thing.

Meanwhile, ducks ply the waters,
waggling through rippled reflections of trees,
turning this way and that, damp beaks shining.
I watch them for a while.

My mind rambles off somewhere.
When it returns, the ducks are gone.
I spot them across the water,
brown quivers and trembles among the roots,
the thousand greens of the island.
They preen and shake their feathers,
rise up on points, fan wings
before settling into the reflections.

The ducks head back from the island,
moving toward me through mirrored trees,
blue of mirrored sky, working little elbows,
orange oars under the surface.

God appears. A modern person
might say it differently.
God does appear,
though not by expectation.

Riding Forth

Another pilgrim,
Parsifal, let the reins lie slack
on his horse's neck,
let the animal carry him
to the realization of his life.

Riding my own animal forth
into this spring morning,
I choose the usual path
with the usual result.

I know, though, the way
the sky is purple with storm
which any time may come,
I, too, must let the reins go slack.

The Trees

I come, this morning, to a place of trees,
trees like family you choose
when the family life chose for you
cannot do what families
are supposed to do.

Joggers trot past.
Dogs exercise their humans.
People picnic, fisherman cast lines.
Lovers kiss in cool shadows
these trees create.

Spring after spring is born.
The Great Wheel turns.
Death comes near,
takes some small creature, goes on.
The trees remain.

Among these trees, I rest in the presence
of what stays strong when storms sweep in,
endures harsh winters at water's edge,
is sheltering, steady,
ever here.

Dialogue

Such yearning.
So much green.
Even the crabapples.
Green.

> Don't you see
> your own life
> is beautiful?

> Don't you see
> the world
> is a mirror of yourself?

> Don't you see
> your spirit burns with the same green fire
> that breathes through the leaves?

SUMMER INTO AUTUMN

City and Lake

Every day, I walk this narrow strip
of sand and rock between the city,
with its worldly concerns,
and the spiritual lake.

Oh, I know, city and lake
would not speak of themselves
like that. I know
I am speaking of myself.

Body, like city, worldly,
brought me here this morning
to admire across the water
towering steel, stone, glass,
showplace of the elegant,
the fiercely achieving.
Body takes satisfaction in that.

Lake, like spirit, impersonal,
elemental, deep,
was here before body built itself
and all this splendor,
will be here after body
and all this splendor
perish.

August Again

There is wisdom in this August
I never before knew with my bones.

Ripeness, always in August, perhaps,
but the full fields lying majestic and blessed,
dappled with sweeping clouds,
were not me, yet,
though August once welcomed me,
warmed me with her embrace,
led me pale and budding
into the cycle of seasons.

Sweetness in this August,
sweet as peach juice flooding sunny cheeks,
streaking to elbows, dripping off lips,
fingers, chins, as we picnic.

In this clearing,
dignity of leaves, grasses
confident of life's green goodness,
now that it's August again.

After Two Weeks with Mary Oliver

The young Bach was so sustained,
drank so deeply of the river
flowing from the mighty
cathedral organ Buxtehude played,
those twelve weeks in Lübeck,
that every note ever after he inscribed
to the glory of God.

A revered teacher can make that happen,
can so open your awareness
you go out every morning
looking for nothing less than an epiphany.

Never again do you pass your eyes
with indifference over the ducks—
those dark silhouettes in the dawn lagoon
trailing golden streaks of fire
through a forest of reflected trees,
between twin suns,
one sun moving steadily up the sky,
one falling to earth,
spreading its dazzle
directly at your feet.

Storm

Late! The sky has been up for hours
working on a storm.
There's sure to be drama at the shore
so I hurry out to the pier
and sit among iron pilings,
ripped and rusting cables.

I look up into huge waves
hurling themselves over stones,
leaping high, sweeping along the pier,
changing from foam to something like glass,
streaking almost to my feet.

Everything turns to dazzle.
Sun glitters blown foam,
makes golden green curling, translucent water
before it crashes. Sky, pale before,
grows intensely blue.
Swept gulls flash and sparkle wings.

As fast as it came the dazzle fades,
becomes sound—rasping shriek of gulls,
wild barking of dogs for no other reason
than the waves, through which the dogs
plunge and surface like porpoises.

Then hiss and rhythmic rumble
of tons and tons of water pounding,
thundering wind.

Dazzle again,
over a thin, long seawall,
onto the tall beacon tower
far out amid all that bright silver,
those white and whirling birds.

This could be any sea.
This could be the first morning.

I could happily
begin, and end, here.

Concerning the Kingdom of God

Sun pouring fire-fall
into the lagoon,
the awakening island luminous.

Golden water blessed by ducks;
on lawns, sparrows
chanting morning devotions.

Horse chestnut trees,
hundreds of little quilted purses open,
offering gleaming mahogany seeds.

We can see it.
We need only
to look.

Belmont Harbor

Eighteen days of August gone,
yet the sun, glinting off the lake,
even this early in the day
is hot on my throat, intense.

I clamber down.
Rocks, all angles and surfaces,
huge, tumbled, partially submerged,
are softened by streaming mosses
moving with swells. Beneath the surface,
green stones tremble, shapeshift.

Something distant stirs: A single wave
moves steadily in and plashes.
The small sound echoes in the overhang.

Off shore, two posts, tempered by waves
and time, reflect: How good to endure,
to partake of all that has happened here.
Even the storms.

The Buddha would say:
All life is sorrowful. Let it drop away.

But oh, the tumbled stones.
Green mosses streaming.
Fishermen, lines in the water.
Boats heading out from harbor.

At Water's Edge

Mist. Everything damp
after last night's downpour.
More to come: Air a saturated sponge.

With all this wet, get right down
to the lagoon. Become a citizen
of water. Be among water birds.

How easily they move about their world,
doing duck things—calling in hollow voices,
preening, flaring wings, upending for food,
churning water.

How comical they are
as they heave themselves onto the path,
waddle toward the grass, turn back,
then, graceful again, slip into the water,
at one with their world.

End of Summer

The colors, grown vivid, extravagant, assured,
are like a woman of the world
who has long since lost her reticence.

No more the Impressionist palette.
This is Calder. Vlaminck.

Yet even now,
in the midst of all this satisfaction,
beds of flowers are dreaming
seed pods, dry leaves, brittle stems.
I sense along the branches
already loosening of the green.

Then
the plain
the lean
the bone.

Autumn Haze

Stepping out this morning
I discover dissolution
everywhere, the air
full of particles.

Bits of things seem to have disengaged
from whatever engaged them yesterday.
Setting out alone, they drift,
catching the light.

It happens to me.
The self begins to scatter.
Whatever I was
adds to the haze.

AUTUMN INTO WINTER

Painterly

From where I sit, the seawall
arcs around the lagoon,
sweeps toward a far gray bridge.
Reflected rounds of trees
line either side.

I want a painter's language
to say how vertical strokes
create the seawall: Burnt sienna,
terra cotta dulled by brown.

A solitary rower, boat a dragonfly,
reaches two thin yellow posts,
hovers, turns. I wonder what he sees,
resting his arms. Our eyes catch briefly.
He skims away, oars fanning out at the ends:
Chinese red.

The wall I want you to see
might have been made
by gathering a strip of pale beige silk,
binding it, dipping one tightly folded edge
into umber dye, the other into olive green,
then spreading the fabric. Streaks of color
near the yellow posts are widely spaced,
but where the creases deepen,
colors come quickly, one upon another.
Beyond the wall, a barrel for trash:
Alizarin crimson.

The greens require study. Variants of jade,
deep emerald edged with silver.

Savor this
before autumn
adds its shading.

Basics

I stand beside the lagoon,
below the bridge. An ordinary place.
Here are basics:
Odd, even.
Dark, light.
Life,—

Look. A fin like a keen blade
slices the surface.
Line.

A fish, throat and belly white,
pushes up, lips open, drops.
Circle.

Again. Lift, drop.
Circle encounters circle.
Bubbles wobble up, break.
Many circles.

Three swans, Magi to Bethlehem,
slowly pass.
Odd.

Two suns (even).
One sun flames among leaves;
one splashes onto the surface.
Fire, water.

A bridge reflects twin selves,
one bright, the other shadowed.
Light, dark.

The fish, motionless now,
hangs by pinkish lips swollen with wanting,
like human lips begging to be kissed.
It stirs, gasping at what waits—
death.

Melancholy

The journey this morning takes me
to the zoo, to the raptor, plunderer,
Strix nebulosa, a solitary great gray owl.
I sit on a little hill across from its cage
large enough for an entire dead tree
to stand upright; not large enough for flying.

Owl and I look at one another.
Our feathers blow, a light rain falling
the way, in the Bible, it falls alike
on the just and the unjust.
Owl is large, as owls go,
eyes much like my own.

The zookeeper explains, by way of a sign,
the world of the great gray owl has been destroyed
by factories, condominiums, shopping malls.
Owl is a wingbeat from extinction.
As if to contradict, owl stretches its wings.
How broad they are, how powerful
they must have been in the wild.

Owl turns to watch, and I watch
as bald eagle, in an adjoining cage,
spreads mighty wings a moment, closes them,
hops to a lower branch.

Three pigeons fly up
over the mesh and away.

I wonder what owl thinks,
if owls think such things,
how squirrel comes casually into the cage
and, casually, leaves.

Chill

I go out
early into the world.

Something inside me
keeps insisting
it's time to die.

I've heard that argument before.
By now I know
how not to get trapped in a metaphor.

My body is not what needs to die.
But a death is definitely called for.

    A death of what?

Duty.
Duty to everything
not my life.

Essentials

I go far out onto the pier,
to nothing but water,
breathing sky,
light like fire.

And silence, out of which
all elements arise,
into which they fall away.

The dark trawler
passes, left to right.
Gone.

Pour everything out.

Open for inpouring.

Offering

Morning after morning
I return to the same place
near the lagoon,
to the dark trees of the island,
to ducks, dogs,
other celebrants of daybreak,
the same sun over water.

Morning after morning
I pour my body
into the ever-burning fire,
the world,
as you do,
all of us do,
inexhaustible offering.

Illumination

The path of illumination
begins at our feet
and shimmers all the way
to the horizon
where something happens
we cannot see.

The last morning
will probably be
much like this.

But then
we will step onto the path
and will not stop.

About the Artists

Carolyn Kelley Williams, a founding member of the performance ensemble *World Enough & Time,* appeared for many years with fellow-poet Zoe Keithley and flutist Kathy Kelley-Hahn offering original poetry and music programs in Midwestern theatres, churches, and cabarets. Many of the poems included here were performed with flute and percussion accompaniment as part of these programs. In 1991, she attended a workshop with Mary Oliver at Bennington. Her work has appeared in *Poet Lore*, *Silo* (Bennington College), and *Primavera*. A Journal Consultant for the Progoff *Intensive Journal* program since 1991, Kelley has presented *Intensive Journal* workshops throughout the US. For more than thirty years, she was managing editor of several international scientific publications.

The present volume is a love-letter to Lincoln Park, along the magnificent shore of Lake Michigan in Chicago, where she lived for more than forty years. In 2012, she moved to Arizona with her husband, Fred Hodges, where she continues writing, teaching, and creating stained glass art.

Artist Lily Gaines has created the original water color illustrations of Chicago's Lincoln Park that are included here. She seeks her subject, from the mundane to the spectacular, with an eye for the light cast on a building, the reflection on a body of water, or the action or activity within her environment. For her, everyone and everything is a story. A self-taught artist, Lily has extensive experience in arts management and program direction for cultural organizations.

Acknowledgements

Thanks to Zoe Keithley and Jean Feraca for their intelligent editorial attention.

Thanks to Lily Gaines for her sumptuous images of Chicagoland in its glory.

Thanks to Jason Grubb of Photowerks, who photographed Lily's paintings.

Thanks to Amy Minato for writing *Hermit Thrush*, giving me an image of excellence, and to Amy's sister, Jenny Koll, for sending me *Hermit Thrush* as a loving gift.

Thanks to Masha Shubin for her gorgeous design, and to Jeremy Solomon and Sahara Peterson for opening the publication door so graciously.

Thanks to Mary Oliver for telling me, at that workshop at Bennington, that to be a true poet one must write poems every day, prompting me to go out at 5:30 every morning looking for an epiphany. Especially, thanks to Mary Oliver for her eternal poems.

Thanks to my beloved husband, Fred Hodges, for our beautiful life together, for making it so sweet, and for welcoming each freshly-caught poem, still flopping about and raw after my early morning visits to the shore.

Thanks to my supportive, gifted friends—you know who you are—for providing an atmosphere where creativity is nourished and affirmed.

And thanks to all who read these poems, for I know you share the path of illumination and pour your own inexhaustible offering into the sacred, ever-burning fire, the world.

www.ingramcontent.com/pod-product-compliance
Lightning Source LLC
Chambersburg PA
CBHW042232090526
44587CB00006B/155